This book belongs to:

____

Made in the USA
Middletown, DE
02 January 2020